Poetry for Wild Spirits

Penny Reilly

ISBN 978-0-6455841-0-3
Poetry for Wild Spirits
Copyright © 2022 Penny Reilly

Published by... Beyond the Gate Studio

Author Penny Reilly

Text and verse, Penny Reilly

Interior art and design, Penny Reilly

Cover design and art, Penny Reilly

Editor, Penny Reilly

Poetry
for
Wild Spirits

Penny Reilly

Dedication

This little volume is dedicated to those who follow the
pathway into the unknown... through the roots of trees, the silk of
corn, the dark depths of ancient forests
and through the valleys of lost and found.

May you find your truth in nature.

Introduction

A Bandrui... a Druid Bard, my life and calling comes through the inspiration I find in the Wild Spirits of nature and through the practise of animism.

As the wheel of the year and seasons turn through their natural cycles and, when as humans, we fall off that wheel, we lose touch with the magick that dwells in all things and in all sentient life, including our own.

Seasons don't move in a straight line, they are fluid and circular, leading one into another, seamlessly. Only humankind see their lives as straight lines, from birth to death and yet, so many times we change our mind, deviate from the original plan, cycling back to another starting point or rush to the end of something before it's truly begun. We wear ourselves out with this concept of time. Look around in nature... there are no straight lines and no clocks.

Animism is the practise of seeing all life as sentient and animate, each with its own character and spirit... no two the same, for no two humans are either. Each creature... each leaf, stem, flower, pod, bark and individual species are not the same but unique... all are one.

So in my world the first step is to connect to 'Genius Loci,' the Spirit of Place and to call on this deep, earth energy for communication, experiences within the realms of nature and a continued growth in understanding how this realm of vast energy works, i.e. via the seasonal changes and cycles as they unfold, all apparently without 'instruction,' rather through a seeming, 'rightness' of moment, an intuitive knowing. For if all life is sentient, animate, then there is an underlying knowing as to when the first buds appear, the first bird sings, the first creature emerges from its winter burrow.

This little volume expresses the wonderful energies that live and play in nature... Penny Reilly, 2022.

Mystery & Healing

We all experience times in our life... naturally occurring periods in any life-cycle, when we fail to understand that endings are simply precursors to new beginnings.

When our life rhythm moves us, into and through these dark times and often, only with the benefit of hindsight, we realise that it is in actuality, a time of mystery, wisdom and great, healing power.

A Million Stars

Each moment
a journey
Every second
a million stars are born
A microcosm of the macrocosm
seconds, minutes
an hour, a day
in time-lapse accuracy
through science
on display
for all to see
No realm of fantasy
can describe
the wonder of this

Journeys
through, within, without
beyond, before
...and nature
land, sea and shore
the evolutionary mirror
of those journeys
...through time
while every soul
the mirror of the stars
that at birth
with each incarnating soul
...align

Listen

Listen...
She will dream soon
Autumn lends colour
Shapes and shadows merge
in twilight gloom
While she sleeps
...in the dream
multi-petaled flowers bloom
Listen...
their colours hold sounds too
Deep tones of red
Cooling tones of blue
At the break of dawn
when wind-blown leaves
rustle
across an emerald lawn
and bird-song greets the day
in a blush of rain-soaked grey
follow her song
along the winding deer trods
...find The Way

Dark & Light

Dark
endorses light
when it flashes, bright
shooting stars
...across a night sky

Light
endorses dark
when it fades
in a shadowed arc
...of filtered colours

Night
endorses day
when it allows
the sun's display
...to mute the very stars

Day
endorses night
returning
specks of light
...to an inky backdrop

Walk Softly

There is a place
that we can go
beyond the muddy
tales of woe
where waters pool
in depths that glow
with dreams of hope
renewing
Where bee-sung songs
drone of peace and plenty
bird chorus' sings
of a life never empty
with nature's rhythm
gently flow
barely rippling the grass
...walk softly

All Things Pass

Life is awareness
in layers of being
birth to death
seeing
renewal of life
and being
Excepting
all things pass
Some
wide-eyed
on sweet
green grass
Effortlessly
fearlessly
the last breath's hiss
releasing
we can learn
...from this

Emergence

Hollowing out
emptying
seeking
the purpose of life
in simply being
Giving up
the fight for more
allows
unhindered
flow
Just living
with no place left
to go
Past
present
future
merges
the well of life
upsurges
the wheel spins
on and around
All places
all seasons
emerge
...as sacred ground

Perpetual Flow

Perpetual flow
rolling in
season to season
Blessed days
of sunshine
rain and shadow
reflected
in how
we walk our way
through emotional
waters deep
or rivulet shallow
and exhausted
dive
immersing self
in life
and grounded
let seeds fall
...in fields, once fallow

I Saw

I saw stars shine
through an overlay of misty cloud
I heard the wind sigh
trees danced to its rhythm
I felt the earth shift
a new season approached
leaves fluttered, branches moaned
Must we retreat, must we let go
our tenuous hold on autumn
but as leaves are released
from their
photosynthesistic journey
colours begin their change
to match
the softer morning light
Breath held, I smell
the musty approach
of winter
when soon enough
dew-besprent grasses
bow their heads
under naked trees
where fungi bloom
and silent owl flight
...calls the season home

Ebb and Flow

Light prisms glisten
Her frost-feathered wings unfurl
spreading white across the ground
Autumn-shadowed leaves curl
fading to dust
bringing nutrient, life and lust
to next year's seeds
...sleeping now
as their needs ebb and flow
no longer the urge to grow
until in spring the surge
of returning life and light
awakens them
from the deep, dark

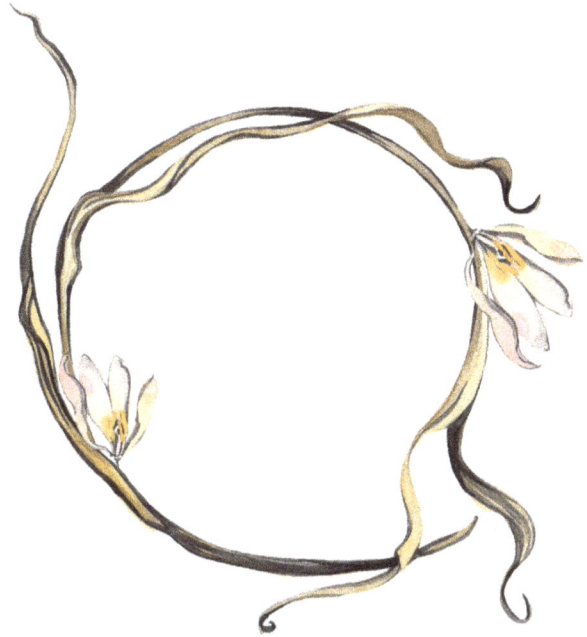

of earth's wintry night
where bright, coloured leaves splice
in amber, green and gold
and gems of ice, glisten
across an emerald lawn
in shades of a limpid dawn
Another year fades
grows old
and in the moonlit glades
her frost-feathered wings unfurl
while humans curl
by glowing fire
...behind closed shades

A Blip

Our natural state
of being
is magick
Moving between
full, exhilarant joy
and oft, comedy tragic
Spaces between
filled with
liquid notes sublime
in cycles spinning
adhering
to nature's rhyme
Diaphonous, silken threads
stretched
on the loom of time
fading
in and out
annual, bianual, diurnal
We are but a blip
...in life eternal

Patterns in the Dark

Patterns
in the spinning wheel of time
Countless messages
hidden within the rhyme
Dancing creatures
live inside the tale
flying in
on seasonal winds
they sail
Living organisms
each with their own ways
follow the ancient rhythm
of the days
Journeying in
the cycle spins again
beyond Samhain and the dark
where lies the ancestry of men
Secret codes
hidden in the night
the language of the stars
pulls us toward the light
yet oft, it's in the darkness
dreams unfold
in shining webs of passion
...like liquid gold

Awen

Sow the seeds
Weave the web in time
Weave
sow
grow
in wisdom
knowledge
of the
life stream
and the
souls spark
of intelligence
Breath
all one
...Awen

Pledge

A pledge to nature, every day
Summer reaches her peak
branches sway
Dandelion clocks
spin their truth in time
while humming, bee-song
breaks the silence
of nature's rhyme
No reason here, just is
the immortal cry
Wild Spirits wait
Wake up they call
In forests deep, they've waited long
emerging now from sleep
Wake up they sing
too late
as silken silence fell
the drum beat ceased
No more
the bird-song bell
A pause
A breath
before
life's final
...death knell

Don't Rush

Don't rush
into your day
Don't push
long-held dreams away
for all the
should do
could do
leaving no space
for you
Be aware
walk softly
...dare
to say no
Be in awe
as winter thaw
runs in rivulets
of melting snow
and bees drone
their spring song
silent
for cold months long
Don't wait
live the moment fully

Let non-existing time flow
as if there were
...no place left to go

Dance

Dance lonely earth child
Dance with the wind
Follow the music
to where magick begins
Sway in the treetops
Sink in the earth
Wade in the tide-lands
of birth and rebirth
Drink in a sunrise
bathe in sunset
Live this earth-life fully
less at death you forget
you are one with all creatures
and this cycle of life
Leave those weapon-thoughts
behind you
let go all strife
Be at one with all nature
free as the wind
Follow the music
...to where magick begins

Drink Time

Wander
where you will
Time
is not something to kill
Drink
the light and shade
in dappled glade
Sip
reflected dew
on sun-drenched
grassy blade
Breath deep
the sun
that dips and fades
behind the hills
...at dusk

Wild Spirits

When I close my eyes
there is peace
All fears fade
anxieties cease
In the innermost forest
where my soul abides
there is music playing
A symphony resides
When my eyes are open
it's all still there
senses heightened
empathic
fully aware
Nature fills these spaces
with healing sounds
subtle smells
birds share my soul-song
sweet chiming bells
Light and shadow are one
here my wild-self dwells
for between
every heart beat
eye blink
each breath

lies the winding pathway
between life and death
The liminal space
on the edge
on the brink
We've slept til now
many
into forgetfulness sink
but it's time to awaken
to remember
who we are
before our wild-self faded
diminished
as if it journeyed far
and yet, we didn't travel
we didn't journey anywhere
merely slept
quietly waiting
the awakening
of Wild Spirit
...slumbering there

There May I Dream

I can feel it
deep in my womb
like sap rising
from an empty tomb
Stirring peacefully
no battle
Freed from
the death rattle
of frosty grip on soil
and musty leaves
that spoil
in sundrenched glade
Budding, new leaves
providing shade
for stag and doe
to lie beneath
Antlers
shedding-swords, unsheathed
as spring's anthem
the calling birds bequeath
There, to the sky
I turn my face
Moss-covered arms
a soul embrace

In sun or moonlight beam
...there may I dream

Wild Places

Wild places
in our heart
fueled by joy and pain
in equal measure
fear and pleasure
Wild places
Woodland ways
offering solitude
and peace
for all our days
Wild places
wind-blown nights
surging power
hiding secret lights
Codes of ancient memory
written in the dark
in the wild places
...of our heart

Renewed

When spring returns
there will be scents
of earth renewed
I'll walk the soil
feet frozen
by the icy
morning dew
I'll share the sun
as birds salute the day
from treetop high
in morning light
and when day ends
I'll sleep the sleep
of peace
as warmth returns
with every passing night
Days will lengthen
bird chorus my alarm

as sunlight streams
my senses
are disarmed
for in the dawn
nightmares
fade and die
I'm filled with the joy
of simple things
and with contentment sigh
When spring returns
I"ll raise my face
to the sun
I'll stand again in icy
morning dew
and like
the earth's
new day begun
...I'll be renewed

Sparrow

Grey skies
Rustling leaves
Sparrow sleeps
beneath the eaves
Sunlight filters
green and gold
...another year grows old
Wild winds
drenching rain
Spirit's gift
brings life again
to haunted hill
and rushing stream
under sunlit day
or bright moonbeam
Visual beauty
growth and demise
creating harmony
under stormy skies
Fragrant blooms
and sour decay
Intrinsic parts
of living
...natures way

Healing

Dappled light
beneath soft green
Where birds cease flight
to roost the night
and sleeping
float
in Autumn's dream
...of healing

Warmth and shelter
shade and cooling
from heat that swelters
in shadowy, willow-weeping
and sleeping
float
in autumn's dream
...of healing

Shadows fall
in moonlit glade
peace overall
in evening, deepening
and sleeping
float
in autumn's dream
...of healing

Hollow Hills

A light shines within the hollow hills
if you may believe in truth
An entry to the realms of Fae, I'm told
but none have returned with proof
For wander, you might
on a moonless night
and never again find the way
as madness creeps
into human blood seeps
until sanity, remembers the day
when in innocence you found
your way underground
and in light and shadow played
Then in joy and desire you played with fire
you were enticed, you dallied, you stayed
Is destiny then, the ruler of men
or do we have our own voice
When darkness invades and daylight fades
do we even have a choice
or is conscience the leveller
that orders the day
as our darkest dreams
...lead us ever astray

Stories

Stories
vagrant memories
assault the senses
Was it real or a dream
are memories as they were
or as they now seem
Fragments
love stories to ancestors
lost in time
triggered by fragrances
Lilac, Rosemary
Sage and Thyme
Humble wild flowers
long, wild
childhood hours
Bees buzzing
an oak tree swing
Crickets hum
while blackbirds sing
All as real as yesterday
Those dear ones
departed
the ancestors
are with us
...everyday

A New Star

There's a new star in the sky tonight
forging an untrodden path in the firmament
Shifting planets, swerve to avoid
her focused, determined journey
to remembering the truth of all that is
as she chases dreams, only imagined
Dancing with intent... finding her Tribe
Moving to the heart beat drum
of the ancestors
Waking, fully aware
honouring her earthly roots
she can stretch higher now
Anchored, she can touch those stars
without floating away into forever
She can hold the consciousness
of the Elders, until life calls her back
to walk her hills and forests again
Remembering the pathway home
...is always, wherever she is

Vale Lyndall Joy Quinn
30th March 1957 - 13th March 2022

Winter

Sun sinks in vibrant colours
Moon rises, white and cold
Sun follows, bursting skyward
in glowing veils of liquid gold
Trees shiver, tender leaves fall
floating gently to the ground
Underfoot, in swathes of colour
creatures wander... snuffling sounds
Night falls, bats and moths fly
Owl, wings her way between
taking only what she needs now
before soaring, sight unseen
All the sounds of nature's quiet time
rustling leaves, a solitary bird
Winter's light, mist-faded, dappled
Be still, listen
...her inner voice is heard

Silent Heart

Her heart is silent
Soul-wings, now frail
She heals the suffering of others
and in turn will fail
but she will find her way
to the edge of time
hearing the night calls
following the rhyme
and rhythm of life
as it ebbs and flows
to the circle of stones
where the Magick knows
all the answers hidden
deep in her soul
She will find her way
to the edge of time
remembering
knowing grows
Illusion falls away
...her soul-light glows

Rebirth

You are this
Your pulse, pumping blood
the hiss
of molten lava, over rock
a kiss
You are water dripping
from ancient trees
You are the overwhelming prayer
that brings you to your knees
You are the bliss you seek
the knowledge you keep
the earth's loamy soil
even molds that spoil
uneaten food

You are the storms that brood
You are the secrets held in ancient stones
Ancestral riddles in a cairn of bones
Soil reveals the DNA
Naked bones are on display
Secrets hidden in millenia past
Slow to decay... bones will outlast
all but the rocks
the bones of earth
In this pulsing rhythm
they renew
...rebirth

Journey in Alignment

Each moment
a journey
Every second
a million stars are born
A microcosm of the macrocosm
seconds, minutes
an hour, a day
in time-lapsed accuracy
on display
for all to see
No realm of fantasy
can describe
the wonder of this

Journeys
through, within, without
beyond, before
and nature
land, sea and shore
the evolutionary mirror
of those journeys
through time
While every soul
the mirror
of the stars
that at birth
with each
incarnating soul
...align

Let Go

In the mists of time
when all made sense of the rhyme
there's a sound that streams
like endless dreams
passing in notes sublime
Who are they
who walked the Old Way
You can hear them still
put your ear to the hill
you'll hear
the wild music they play
Rhythms grow
the trees dance and blow
in an unseen wind off the heath
Drums rumble
summoning from beneath
The earth splits wide

pouring out, the Fae ride
Their songs they do bequeath
Walk softly, they sing
Let joy your notes bring
to a world that is cold
a world grown old
Let go your fears
Treasure passing years
Let go, no need to cling
Joy will return
Bellies fed, passion burns
as their music slowly returns
Let your feet, tap and glide
while their gentle notes slide
Fill to the brim
...your soul that yearns

A Wistful Song

Seasons change
the year moves on
Listen closely
in the forest
there's a wistful song
though it's fading now
as windswept skies
blow a covering of leaves
over where she lies
to sleep away
the chilly hours
in woodland glade
and dappled bowers
Small creatures flock
to see her there
tying feathers and flowers
in her fading hair
They watch her sleep
and wait for spring
when once again
...they'll hear her sing

Lady of the Flowers

Lady of the Flowers
in her sun-drenched bowers
will soon, just fade away
Without our prayers, beliefs and faith
she will disappear, become a wraith
So much will be lost
that can set us free
As a pale moon rises
come dance with the Sidhe
Feel the wind on your skin
to laugh is no sin
For there's more to life
than the chink of loose change
There's a song that spins
every thread to rearrange

So feel the pace quicken
the drum beats sound
calling you to dance
into the open faerie mound
You'll not be lost
it's just a little way from here
A place to play
and let go all fear
for without our prayers, hopes
and dream today
the Lady of the Flowers
...will simply fade away

Watery Kin

Watery depths
of ocean and lake
call your innermost
soul-tides to awake
To float in her darkness
both salty and sweet
riding her waves
to the shores of deep sleep
Life is her gift
through the blood in your veins
and in the lymph fluid
flowing gently
to pool and drain
through every cell
and under your skin
Swim in her depths
find your tail
grow a fin
In her dark pools seek
...find your watery kin

Elen of the Ways

There's a gentle sound from the forest
and a fragrance on the air
Elen walks the Deer Trod Ways
with wild, unruly hair
In autumn's shortening, golden days
antlers rear from her forehead fair
Unknown to many, she's the silent one
with depths untold, to share
Ancient, forgotten, she now returns
to find you, when your search is done
and life is lived with care
She teaches of the forest ways
of living wild and free
where life abounds untold
then you'll hear her whispering
in your dreams
and feel her arms enfold
Let go...
there's nothing left to do
but be
...her non-resisting child

In Silence

In silence
dawn breaks
in the wee small hours
Lights flicker behind my eyes
Dreams visiting
in the guise
of morning
where I walk
on dew-soaked ground
free of care
No longer mortal-bound
Weightless
bathed in a soothing light
Drifting
Soul-freedom in flight
Then, music splits the fear
of the long, dark night
in two

My ghostly self and mortal I
once more inseparable
and life aware
Senses return
Subtle aromas float
on moist, cool air
Autumn-russet tones
shake the leaves
rattling, stirring
ageing bones
yet, bathing the treees
in colour
and sighing in pleasure
I turn another page of my book
A new day
in a cosy nook
Dawn breaks anew
...in the wee small hours

The Greening

We walk the Wildlands
of the Between
searching each being
for a heart that is seen
to care about life
and a love of The Green
...only then, do we share
our knowledge, unseen
The depths of The Greening
are yet to be reached
the rules of life
have been sorely impeached
but as teachers, we roam
in hope to find
souls who are ready
to expand their mind
Walk with us, dance with us
around the silver wheel
The Lady walks with you
she teaches you to feel
truly, deeply
as soul-memory returns
and you find
in the silent wildwoods
...that for which, your soul yearns

I Am

I am the mist in droplets bright
that drift across the moor
I am the rain, in lashing spite
battering at your door
I am the murmer of a sleeping child
I am the scent in a forest wild
I am the sigh of lovers in their bed
the music growing in your head
that has your wits beguiled
I am autumn glow and winter freeze
my love can bring you to your knees
in the warm glisten
of a grandmother's eyes
I am candlelight
even after the flame dies
I am a fish that swims
in pools of water deep

the shadowy dreams
in your troubled sleep
I am the words that whisper
"forget your pain today"
I am a fragile pair of wings,
calling you to play
I am the fragrance
of a bright new morn
the first sound you made
at the moment you were born
I am the sun that warms your skin
a moonbeam of silver thread to spin
for we are one in energy, we are kin
I am a blade of grass
a slender dancing tree
I am your Wild Spirit
...I set you free

In Circle Round

In circle round
on shing Tor
a fragrance lingers
swept 'cross the moor
where rippling streams
tumble over stones
and in Circle cast
Old Ways are known
Herbs of reason
and sound intent
burned in sacred fires
now spent
when wise ones knew
the language of trees
and no mortal, to another
bent their knees
Intuitive yes
primitive, no
Walk the shining pathway
...into the gossamer flow

Standing Stones

Stone lintels
a church of sorts
perhaps invisible, open ports
to other realms
Scents evocative
not of myrrh and frankincense
rather, honeysuckle-sweet
intense
Subtle, illusive doors
a track, through landscapes clean
'cross fragrant moors
where standing stones
honouring ancient rights
find balance
between Equinox days
Solstice nights
A scent of mist
of woodlands green
paying tribute to
a pantheon of faceless gods
or offerings
...to the Great Unseen

Magick Walks

Magick walks
before daylight stalks
the night
Shadow creeps
where moonlight seeps
into
the cracks of dawn
Faded flowers
with drooping heads
drop petals
on dampened beds
edged by emerald lawn
beneath which
stirring creatures yawn
smoothing damp, ruffled fur
with moistened tongue
the dewy drops that clung
through sleep
while in hollows deep
Magick walks
and moonlight stalks
...the dawn

Moon-shadowed

I dreamed of a creature
with moon-shadowed eyes
Her hair all a'tangle
a Fae in disguise
She smiled at me fiercely
revealing white teeth
then opening her wings
flew away o'er the heath
I awoke with a start
the sun on my face
What had I witness
I felt blessed with grace
The next night was the same
her eyes violet; aflame

She tugged at my sleeve
whispered my name
and again I woke up
but the sunlight was gone
all that was left
was a soft, fragile song
I pondered and wondered
who the creature might be
the reply came so fast
"Why I'm you and you're me"
I dreamed of a creature
a Fae in disguise
and I looked in the mirror
...at my moon-shadowed eyes

Longest Night

A day dawns bright
longest night is done
Shadows creep
yet, in the deep
winter's grip soon gone
Light returns
darkness spurns
the shining light of day
In the deep
stirring from sleep
green shoots begin display
A warbling bird
on a gloomy day heard
when all else is still
is a sound so sweet
even without sun's heat
brings warmth
to my windowsill
Crocus thrust
through the earth's cold crust
lilac buds show green
Within the deep
earth stirs from sleep
...beauty in the mist I've seen

Magickal Child

Wonder at the child
who remembers the land
Walk with her
through the twilight
let her take you by the hand
Watch as her face
lights up with bright joy
Life is simple for her
and nothing can destroy
her delight
as she witnesses
nature spirits glide
Fae folk flit through trees
while water spirits slide
down cascading streams
Multi-coloured moonbeams
light the way
No darkness dwells
in her midnight dreams
We don't need to teach her
she already knows
Let her lead you
to those places
...you forget to go

Lightening Bolt

In solitude
I find myself standing
where sea and sand
meet sky
Alone but not lonely
I ponder
the timeless soul
that is "I"
Reflecting
in quiet surrender
realisation came
with a jolt
beyond the difference of gender
came a stray
somewhat lonely, thought
a lightening bolt
We are all one in the centre
Our being
one and the same
Though along different paths
we venture
in solitude we merge
...one flame

Inspiration

Inspiration
can arrive in a moment
or take time to manifest
Appear, in a second of mayhem
or one in quiet rest
Words and images
flow from within
growing in power and sound
Music cascading in wondrous notes
or cacophonous noise to astound
In moments of madness
in depths of despair
Within sanity's reach
or beyond mortal care

Where does it come from
to where does it go
from out of the aethers
deep in the flow
of mystical rhythm
magickal choirs
earthy, deep tones
bright, frenzied fires
Inspiration comes quickly
or, oft times, slow
Listen
feel it pulse
Call it in
...or let it go

Pause

A hush falls
A deadly pause
...then silence
A breath held
music breaks and melds
the pause between
each breath
each beat
of an anguished heart
when body and soul part
When it stutters and dies
is the pause eternal
the silence, silence
or does music guide the soul
with vibrant light and sound
into the pause
between
the long-held breath
...and death

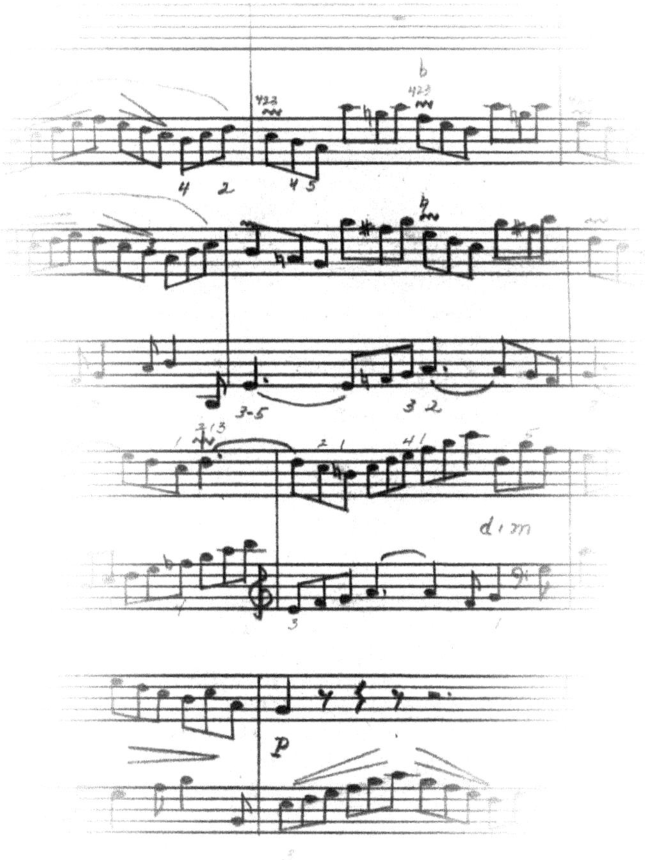
dim

Twilight Dreams

Twilight dreams
shadows merge and blend, unseen
except, where water droplets gleam
in hidden depths of sacred bowers
their scent evocative
after sweet rain showers
cleanse the air
Fragrances of loam and moss
spread upon and under
ancient trees
intoxicate
to bring the wanderer to their knees
in prayers of gratitude
It is here, the wooded ones in disguise
trade their secrets
and all your senses beguile
They wait for you in moonlit glade
preparing you to walk
in dark and light... in subtle shade
For in the shadows
all things are equal in their sight
It is only the human psyche
that fears the dark of night
and yet, without the darkness
...we cannot see the light

Greening Ways

A windswept plain
or a vast ocean deep
are you awake
or do you still sleep
while our world
needs our attention
in these changing days
do you walk the pathway
...of the Greening Ways

Warm winds blow
as the spring air blooms
with fragrant blossoms
scenting rooms
Wild ducks float
on quiet ponds
under a canopy
...of willow wands

Beneath all life
a vibration plays out
when we truly hear
it dispels all doubt
Life is a challenge

a dream, a gift
but we cannot just let
...our planet drift

We can pretend it's alright
stick our head in the sand
Feel her heat like a furnace
consuming the land
scorching grasses
burning trees
but eventually we'll feel
...her ice on the breeze

Earth Mother dreams
but she's stirring now
Again, if you listen
she will show you how
What are your tasks
what roll will you play
for the safe homecoming
...of the Greening Ways

In the Dreaming

Where do you go in your dreaming
Are you sure you're awake
Do you follow your Wild-heart Spirit
or react for reacting's sake
Where are you, when you're dreaming
Is it a peaceful place
Do you go to the lands of plenty
to a Sacred-greening space
How do you feel in the morning
Are you truly here
or are you really still dreaming
'til small whispers of truth appear
Do you dream of a journey
Do you know where to
Is it long and exciting
In the dream are you... you
Does it feel like a memory
written deep in your cells
of an Isle of Apples
and a sweet-water well
Who travels with you
or are you alone
Do you feel like you're lost
...or are you travelling home

Last Dance

Dance the last dance
of dragonfly
on delicate wings
in an azure-blue sky
Soon the mists and frosts
of winter time
will cover the lands
in an icy rime
She will sleep the long sleep
in enchanted pools
her wings, folded tight
while the planet cools
and then in spring
her offspring emerge
to fly trembling again
on the brink
on the verge
for nothing ever
truly dies
as we dance the last dance
...of dragonfly

Changing the Mantle

She's changing her gown
from green to gold
the harvest ripens
as the year grows old
Mabon's first kiss
is felt in the air
as elderberry ripen
in hedgerow fair
What do you wish
for your harvest this year
Have you laboured long
for your fruits to appear
Let go the old growth
let the leaves fall
the fruits of your harvest
...will come when you call

Delicate

She is so small
her wings are frail
Once vibrant green
they're now so pale
She is tired
and needs to sleep
She'll burrow down
into the deep
How will she live
in the smoke and dust
the driving rains
earth's rumbling crust
Where will she go
fragile as snow
As you believe
so is she real
You may not see her
but you can feel
If you say no
she'll simply go
Disappearing
into the flow

Dryad's Dance

Deep in the heart
of the forest green
the Dryads dance
their attendance unseen
Listen to them
Speak with them
as their truths they share
for the tree and the Dryad
are an inseparable pair
They will speak of the Quickening
and what you can do
to keep ahead on your path
staying true
to the mother who birthed you
and the planet blue
Stand up
Take action
Don't sit the fence
YES... that means you

Worlds Within

Worlds within worlds
lives within lives
fly swift as a bird
be a fish as it dives
Smell the soil
burrow deep
Hear the earth
Does she sleep
Nestle in
worming down
be the bug
in the ground
Be a cell in her skin
go within
...deep within

Samhain Ride

The Wild Folk ride
through forest green
Once a year
they're easily seen
they come from beyond
the in-between
...breaking through the Veil
Their horns sound bright
voices light
riding through
the dark of night
with faces... oh so pale
The Wild Hunt rides
hounds by their sides
to chase the dark away
as the Green Lord
comes a'gathering in
those who were led astray
She waits for them
in a lightened glen
where the Fae Folk play
He leads them on
through the forest fair
to the Summerlands
...far away

Wild Lands

Heart of the wildlands
spirits of old
what do you teach us
so gentle yet bold
Whom do you call on
as this new spring breaks
Who will hear you
Who will awake
Will we stay sleeping
or will we wake up
to dance in your meadows
drink from your cup
Will we remember
as time's speeding by
...remember
the Greening
...and fly

Wild Spells

A spell is a wish
a dream, a desire
It needs passion
and courage
to play with fire
that burns
in the belly
...aflame within
allowing the sensations
growing under your skin
Want is not always
enough to create
the power to invoke
a dream to make
It needs more
than a please
or begging for aid
It must burst
from the dark
kindle in the shade
then explode into light
born of truth
...unafraid

About the Author

Penny Reilly

Poet, artist, author, photographer, Penny lives in the Victorian Highlands on a 20 acre retreat-farm, where she has her studio.

Penny, lives a quiet rural life dedicated to her surrounds. A self-sufficient lifestyle in the peace of nature, Penny is the author of nine volumes of both urban fantasy and poetry, which include her art in mixed media, watercolours, goache, hand-made eco-inks and embellished with the little gifts nature provides on her daily walks.

Her work has been exhibited at numerous venues and her love of both the written word and painting is a powerful means of expression.

You can find her at http://pennyreillyartistbeyondthegate.com for her blog and on both instagram and facebook.

Her books are readily available on Amazon, world wide and her art, directly via her facebook or instagram contact details.

Books by the Author

Silver's Threads Book 1
Spinning Colours Darkly 2012

Silver's Threads Book 2
Grey Weavings 2012

Silver's Threads Book 3
Warp and Weft 2013

Silver's Threads Book 4
Silken Web 2014

Silver's Threads Book 5
Skeins of Time 2015

Unfurled
Nature Poetry 2016

Scraps and Wild Gatherings
Short Story Collection 2018

In Stillness
Poetry for Grief and Healing 2020

www.ingramcontent.com/pod-product-compliance
Lightning Source LLC
Chambersburg PA
CBHW051611030426
42334CB00035B/3490